**ENGAGE IN
SPIRITUAL
DISCIPLINES**

# vital: BIBLE STUDY
# GIVING
# SUBMISSION
# GIVING
# THANKS

PHIN HALL

**CWR**

# Contents:

# Introduction:

'Continue to work out your salvation with fear and trembling, for it is God who works in you to will and to act according to his good purpose.'
**Philippians 2:12–13**

At its core, Christianity is about a loving relationship with God. You may have thought it was about attending a church, reading the Bible, doing good deeds or hanging out with other Christians. While such activities are important, this is only as part of our relationship with God. Everything worthwhile in the Christian life stems from our love for God. The more we love Him, the more we will live in a way that glorifies Him.

In marriage, God has given us a wonderful illustration of our relationship with Him. Even if you have never been married the concepts are still simple to grasp. In the very first marriage (see Genesis 2) after God had decided it was not good for Adam to be alone, He made the first woman, Eve, as 'a helper suitable for him' (v.18).

This word 'helper' does not imply a position of inferiority. Eve was to be a partner, a companion, working in a complementary role with Adam. They were commissioned by God to rule over the world and fill it with their offspring. While Adam was responsible for this work, he obviously could not accomplish it on his own – he needed the partnership of his wife! Our relationship with God is also a partnership. Both parties have a complementary role to perform.

In his letter to the Philippian church, Paul called them to 'work out' their salvation whilst encouraging them that God was 'working in' them. The Bible is clear that God's role is to transform us to be more like Christ, changing our hearts to love Him more and so

Free downloadable teaching videos of approximately 5 minutes are available for each week. Scan the QR code or visit the weblink to view.

**INTRODUCTION**

www.cwr.org.uk/vital

increasingly live for Him. For centuries God's people have engaged in practices vital for their relationship with God. We call this 'spiritual discipline': this is *our* role in 'working out' our salvation. In this series we will look at the following seventeen areas of spiritual discipline that have stood the test of time:

+ **Focus on God:** worship, Bible study, meditation and prayer.

+ **Focus on others:** fellowship, submission, serving and witnessing.

+ **Focus on ourselves:** simplicity, giving, battling temptation and fasting.

+ **Focus on daily life:** solitude, silence, giving thanks, confession and living for today.

Practices like these do not make us Christians, but as we work at them, God works with us by transforming us. This must always be our objective in spiritual discipline. If the practices themselves are our goal then spiritual discipline can turn into worthless ritual. Our motivation and desire must *always* be to have our hearts changed – love for God must be the most important thing in our lives, just as it is also the greatest privilege.

In this book we will consider the following four areas: *Bible study, submission, giving* and *giving thanks*. Each week consists of five sessions of individual study, reflection and application. A final session has questions either for personal consideration or group discussion.

My prayer is that these studies will help you as you work out your salvation in partnership with God and so grow in your love for Him.

**1.** Do you believe that Christianity is essentially about a loving relationship with God, and if so, why?

**2.** How would you explain the purpose and practice of Bible study?

**3.** How would you explain the purpose and practice of submission?

**4.** How would you explain the purpose and practice of giving?

**5.** How would you explain the purpose and practice of thanksgiving?

**6.** Which of these have you engaged in previously, and how has doing so helped your spiritual growth?

**7.** Read 2 Corinthians 3:18 and Romans 12:1–2. Our relationship with God involves a partnership. How would you define the role that we play and the role that God plays? Consider your own experience of this partnership.

# WEEK 1: FOCUS ON GOD
# Bible study

## Introduction

'All Scripture is God-breathed and is useful for teaching, rebuking, correcting and training in righteousness.'
**2 Timothy 3:16**

We know this! It is Christianity 101 stuff – the real basics. And whether or not we can explain or defend it, we believe that the Bible is the Word of God. The word 'Scripture' that Paul uses in this verse from 2 Timothy occurs over sixty times in the New Testament, and on every occasion it refers to the writings we have in our Bibles. This collection of sixty-six books is a message from God to us, His people.

Not only do we know all this, but as a result we also know that we should study our Bibles. 'Should', however, does not always give birth to 'do', and the overwhelming evidence of most research tells us this unsurprising fact: the majority of Christians do not study, and rarely even read, the Bible. In our defence, we are not always taught *how* to study the Bible and as a result we tend to become discouraged or confused and eventually give up. Is Bible study more than just scurrying through a few chapters each day? Is it more than reading a page of devotional Bible notes? And is it really as important as Christians make out?

In this first week of studies we will be looking at what Bible study is and why to do it, together with how to engage effectively in this area of spiritual discipline.

## More than Words

> '"What is written in the Law?" [Jesus] replied. "How do you read it?"'
> **Luke 10:26**

When it comes to putting people on the spot, no one compares to Jesus! As He made His way to Jerusalem, an expert in the Law asked Jesus what he had to do to inherit eternal life. But rather than answer the question, Jesus threw it back at him: 'How do you read it?' Obviously Jesus was not enquiring how this man *physically* read the Law, He was after the expert's interpretation – his summary of the message of Scripture ... And he answered well. He had clearly been studying his Bible!

Bible study is more than simply reading the words on the printed page. It involves taking the time to work out and consider what it really has to say – 'How do *you* read it?' This goes by the somewhat grand title of 'hermeneutics' and involves asking questions of the text, such as:

+ what did it mean to the original reader?

+ how might this be relevant to the Church today?

+ what is God specifically saying to me through this?

It is often said that human communication has much less to do with the words themselves than with body language and tone of voice. In fact, words are

*the science & methodology of interpretation esp of Scriptural text*

Bible study

usually credited with only seven per cent of a person's message! No doubt we have all experienced times where our written words have been misinterpreted, or where we have taken other people's letters and emails the wrong way, reading *into* them an attitude or tone that they had not intended. As we only have the words to work with, and none of the other essentials for communication, one of the biggest concerns about the Bible is that it seems so open to interpretation. Is it really possible to work out with any certainty what it has to say to us?

Thankfully we are not working alone or from scratch as we embark on our studies. As we will see, we not only have the Holy Spirit, the Author of Scripture Himself, to guide us and teach us, but we have a wealth of knowledge and study that has been handed down to us through centuries of Church history. There are countless study guides, commentaries, sermon transcripts, Bible notes and suchlike to help us as we wrestle with God's Word, and while the amount of material available may seem a bit overwhelming, other Christians will be able to advise on the study aids that have proved most helpful to them.

# > < Reflection

The preaching of Scripture is a vital part of church meetings – indeed one of the principal roles of church leaders is to teach God's Word. However, it becomes a problem when our *only* source of biblical input is a couple of sermons on a Sunday.

Have a read of the opening verses of Psalm 1 and reflect on the 'blessed' effect of daily Bible study.

**Day 2**

A Message from God

> 'Above all, you must understand that no prophecy of Scripture came about by the prophet's own interpretation. For prophecy never had its origin in the will of man, but men spoke from God as they were carried along by the Holy Spirit.'
> **2 Peter 1:20–21**

Bible study

'The Bible is the Word of God, because it says it is!' While this is something of a circular argument, this is the point we always arrive at when trying to explain our reasons for this belief. And it is, of course, to be expected since, as the Word of God, the Bible is the highest authority on which we can call. To appeal to any other authority, such as reason or scientific evidence, to prove the Bible's claim would be to downgrade the authority of Scripture itself.

There is a great defence of Scripture in the Westminster Confession, which states, in slightly archaic English, 'it doth abundantly evidence itself to be the Word of God: yet notwithstanding, our full persuasion and assurance of the infallible truth and divine authority thereof, is from the inward work of the Holy Spirit bearing witness by and with the Word in our hearts.' In short, as we study the Bible with the help of God, so we are assured that all Scripture truly is God-breathed!

This being the case, there is a general feeling among Christians that we should have read every bit of the Bible at some point in our lives, which has given birth to the 'Bible in a year' movement. Unfortunately, this is liable to engender either a somewhat superficial knowledge of God's Word, or feelings of failure for not keeping up with the challenge. Yet, since *all* Scripture is useful, surely whether we have read every word is not the issue – rather it is the need to ensure we get into the depths of God's Word, not simply the breadth of it.

And we need to do so regularly. When Jesus taught His disciples to pray He said, 'Give us each day our daily bread' (Luke 11:3). While this is primarily a request for the daily provision of our physical necessities, we also read that 'Man does not live on bread alone, but on every word that comes from the mouth of God' (Matt. 4:4).

God has given us His Word so that we can grow to know Him better. As such it is surely worth our time, attention and diligent study as often as possible.

# > < Reflection

Since the beginning, Satan has attacked God's Word with the constant refrain, 'Did God really say...?' (Gen. 3:1) For two thousand years the Bible has come under persistent scrutiny and attack; people have given their lives both for it and against it. Yet through all of this – through Roman persecution and the illiteracy of the Dark Ages, through Scholasticism and the Enlightenment, through 'higher criticism' and the rise of militant atheism – the Bible has stood firm.

'The grass withers and the flowers fall, but the word of our God stands forever.' (Isa. 40:8)

'[Paul] writes the same way in all his letters, speaking in them of these matters. His letters contain some things that are hard to understand, which ignorant and unstable people distort, as they do the other Scriptures, to their own destruction.'
**2 Peter 3:16**

Bible Study

Peter is often portrayed as a bit of a comedy character, quick to blunder in, slow to understand, a simple fisherman caught out of his depth. And while this seems a rather unfair portrayal, he was not afraid to admit that he found some of Paul's writing hard to understand. Yet he still used that term 'Scriptures' to describe Paul's words – Peter considered them the very words of God! And while he found them hard to understand, there is no doubt he would have taken the time to study what Paul had to say and grapple with its complex concepts.

If you have ever found the Bible hard to understand and interpret, you are in good company. There are very few, if any, who find it simple! Because of this it is important to approach Bible study carefully:

**1.** Before reaching for your Bible, *choose a time*. Another book in this series looks at solitude and silence, and these twin disciplines are a great counterpart for Bible study. Choose a time when you can get away from all the noise and distractions to really concentrate and focus on God's Word and the guidance of the Holy Spirit, for however long it takes.

**2.** *Decide what you are going to study.* Try to avoid the temptation to open up your Bible randomly and start reading; instead take the time to choose a book, a biblical character or a topic to tackle. Being faced with over 1,200 chapters in sixty-six books can be somewhat daunting, so ask other Christians what they are studying or make use of daily Bible notes, which tend to work through books rather than jump around, making sure you do your study as well as reading the devotional comments!

**3.** Before picking up the book itself, *take the time to pray.* The Holy Spirit's main work is to guide us into truth – He inspired the Scriptures, so it makes sense to ask Him to guide us as we study.

**4.** At last, it is time to *open your Bible and start reading,* and as you do so, ask questions of the text: 'What does it mean?' 'What message was the writer trying to convey?' 'How might it have been understood by the original reader?' 'What does it say about God?' and so on. This is looked at in greater depth in the study 'Focus on God: Meditation'.

# Application »

As mentioned on Day 1, we have a wealth of 2,000 years' worth of biblical study. Chat with other Christians to see what studies they have found helpful, especially study Bibles and commentaries. It is worth getting hold of some of these to assist you in this area of spiritual discipline.

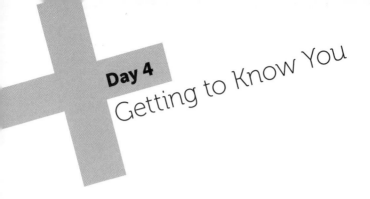

## Day 4
### Getting to Know You

'When he takes the throne of his kingdom, [the king] is to write for himself on a scroll a copy of this law, taken from that of the priests, who are Levites. It is to be with him, and he is to read it all the days of his life so that he may learn to revere the LORD his God and follow carefully all the words of this law and these decrees.'
**Deuteronomy 17:18–19**

Long before Saul took the throne of Israel, God laid out the laws that were to govern the king's life. These included the command to write out his own copy of the law, and whether this referred to the whole Torah or just the book of Deuteronomy, it was certainly no small task! Having done so, the king was to spend time each day reading what he had written, saturating himself with Scripture. Rather than simply delivering the command and leaving it at that, Deuteronomy then gives the reason for the king's devotion to God's Word: 'so that he may learn to revere the LORD his God and follow carefully all the words of this law' – reverence for God and a life pleasing to the Lord.

In the few thousand years since these laws were written, these two goals of Bible study have not changed. We read our Bibles not merely to know what it says, but to be changed by it both inwardly and outwardly. Inwardly our aim is to get to know God, who He is, what is important to Him and how He speaks and acts. The more we discover who God is, the more we will revere Him – honouring Him and loving Him above all else. Outwardly, then, as we grow in this knowledge and love of God, this will shape the way we live – the things we think, say and do.

The Bible is the Word of God; our ultimate authority; the truth, and Jesus declared, 'the truth will set you free' (John 8:32). As we study Scripture, guided and taught by the Holy Spirit, we find freedom through all that it reveals to us about God; freedom not only to love and live for ourselves, but also for God – for His glory and His kingdom.

## Application »

'I hear and I forget. I see and I remember. I do and I understand.' (Confucius)

These three activities may be likened to the hearing, reading and writing down of Scripture. We have already considered writing and reading, and in Romans, Paul wrote: 'faith comes from hearing the message, and the message is heard through the word of Christ' (Rom. 10:17). However, it is not always true to assume that we forget what we hear, remember what we read and understand only what we write. We all learn in different ways. For example, I absorb information best through hearing.

Try experimenting with these three ways of studying Scripture and see which is most effective in helping you understand what is written.

Bible study

> 'Jesus replied, "You are in error because you do not know the Scriptures or the power of God."'
> **Matthew 22:29**

What a damning statement from Jesus! In one of His many run-ins with His fellow Jews, this was His response to a trick question from members of the Sadducees. This elite Jewish sect had great social and political clout in Judea, being well respected and highly regarded for their religious insight and adherence to the Scriptures. And yet Jesus rebuked them for knowing neither the Word nor the power of God!

Since our ultimate aim is to become more like Jesus we will end each week focusing on Him as our ultimate example of how to live a disciplined life. In contrast to the Sadducees, Jesus not only knew the power of God, but demonstrated exceptional knowledge of the Scriptures, quoting them over eighty times in the Gospels.

After His baptism, Jesus spent forty days and nights fasting in the wilderness and being tempted by Satan. He enticed Jesus to break His fast by turning a stone to bread to satisfy His hunger. He offered Jesus a fast-track to kingship in return for His worship. He challenged Jesus to prove He was the Christ by forcing God's hand to rescue Him.

In response, Jesus did not enter into an argument or debate, but instead He countered every attack with the Word of God, quoting Scripture in defence, wielding 'the sword of the Spirit' with devastating precision. Jesus demonstrated how valuable this sort of biblical knowledge and insight can be. Being able to call to mind Scripture to help resist our spiritual enemy is crucial – this is considered further in the study 'Temptation: focus on ourselves'.

Jesus knew the Scriptures so well that when He was walking on the road to Emmaus with a couple of His followers, Luke tells us, '... beginning with Moses and all the Prophets, he explained to them what was said in all the Scriptures concerning himself' (Luke 24:27). An impromptu Bible study through the entirety of the Old Testament, undertaken on a mere seven-mile journey! But being born as a human, Jesus did not automatically know the Scriptures; He had to spend time reading, learning and studying the Bible just like us, while at the same time He was busy fulfilling it!

# > < Reflection

In another run-in with His compatriots, Jesus was accused of breaking the Sabbath law. In response to their legalistic stance, He said, 'You diligently study the Scriptures because you think that by them you possess eternal life. These are the Scriptures that testify about me, yet you refuse to come to me to have life.' (John 5: 39–40)

As we have seen, diligently studying the Scriptures is vital for us as God's people, but at the same time our aim in studying the Bible is not simply to grow in our knowledge of this book, but to grow in our knowledge and love of God.

Bible study

**1.** What, if anything, puts you off studying the Bible?

*it's difficult to understand - so much of*

**2.** If Jesus asked you, like the expert in the Law, to sum up the message of Scripture, what would you say in response?

*The love of God*

**3.** Read John 16:13. The Holy Spirit's main role is to guide and speak to us. Consider times when you have experienced His work in revealing the truth of the Bible to you.

**4.** What aids to Bible study have you found helpful and would you recommend them to others?

*Other knowledgeable people, good sermons. study guides.*

**5.** If you experimented with the three different ways of studying Scripture (hearing, reading and writing – see page 15), which one did you find most effective for understanding? How might you make use of this in your Bible study?

**6.** Have you ever committed passages of Scripture to memory, and if so how has this been beneficial?

**7.** If a Christian friend asked you how to study the Bible, what advice would you give them?

*with a group or study aid*

# WEEK 2: FOCUS ON OTHERS

# submission

## Introduction

'I urge you, brothers, to submit to such as these and to everyone who joins in the work, and labours at it.'
**1 Corinthians 16:15–16**

Submission is not a popular concept these days. It is a word loaded with unhelpful connotations, and is usually defined in the context of giving in to or being overpowered by a superior force or authority.

Take wrestling for instance. Two opponents battle one another with all their might and neither person wants to lose and will not give in easily. It is only the greater strength or ability of one that eventually brings the other to the point of defeat, pinning them down in some unbearably painful hold until they are forced, finally, into submission.

Is this really relevant to spiritual discipline and our interaction with others? Does being a follower of Christ condemn us to a life of giving in to everyone, allowing them to beat and oppress us as they see fit?

As we turn our attention to this second area of spiritual discipline, we will be looking at what submission is really all about – what it involves and why it is so important for us as God's people. We will also consider how to practise submission and how it helps to shape our relationship not only with other people but also with God.

19

# Day 1
## Getting in Line

'Submit to one another out of reverence for Christ.'
**Ephesians 5:21**

submission

The city of Ephesus, which today lies in ruins, was once the great capital of the Roman province of Asia, second only to Rome in size and importance. As such the Ephesians who received Paul's letter would have been very familiar with the Roman way of life – its customs, its politics, its religious practices and so on. They were also very familiar with the Roman army, many legions of which were regularly based in the surrounding countryside.

The Greek word for 'submit' was often used as a military term, having the sense of arranging yourself under your superior officers – getting in rank. The Roman army had a very clear authority structure. At the bottom were the legionaries (the foot soldiers who were the might of Rome) and the average legion had around eleven thousand of them. They were arranged in groups of eighty under the centurions and even the centurions had a pecking order with the leader of the first century having the highest rank.

Above them were the tribunes and other officers, all of whom reported to the legate, the commander of the legion. Even he could not simply do as he wished, but in turn reported to the general who was himself accountable to the emperor and senate back in Rome. By ordering themselves under those who ranked above them, the soldiers of each level would 'submit' themselves, getting in line with everyone else.

Out of reverence for Christ, to whom we ultimately submit, we also are called to get in line with everyone else, not simply taking the place we *feel* we deserve, but choosing to take the lowest place. 'If any man would come after me,' said Jesus, 'let him deny himself and take up his cross and follow me' (Mark 8:34). What could be lower than being sentenced to crucifixion – a death fit only for slaves and outcasts?

In a society where the strongest fight for the highest positions, submission is often thought of as a sign of weakness. In reality, it is quite the opposite. True submission takes great strength.

# Application »

James wrote about people making plans to 'go to this or that city, spend a year there, carry on business and make money' (James 4:13). He went on to point out that no one knows what will even happen tomorrow. Like the rich man in Jesus' parable, our lives could be demanded of us this very night!

One of the biggest fears about dying is all the things in life we will miss out on – all the sights we have not seen, the adventures we have not experienced, the people we have not met or spent sufficient time with. The same fears often underlie our distaste for submission. If we submit to others we may miss out on getting or doing the things we want. Take some time to think how submitting to others may affect the way you live.

'All of you, clothe yourselves with humility toward one another, because, "God opposes the proud but gives grace to the humble."'
**1 Peter 5:5**

submission

Unsurprisingly I was not a model schoolboy. 'This is the worst class I have ever taught!' was a frequent remark from my teachers, and I was the common denominator. Many times I received a clip round the ear for some silly comment, or a ruler across the hand for worse. On one occasion I even had to 'assume the position' to be beaten elsewhere! At the time corporal punishment was in the process of being outlawed in schools, but back then pupils were generally unaware of it. Today, however, school children *know* they cannot be touched – they know their rights, and teachers have to be very careful how they interact with their pupils.

Knowing and even demanding our rights has become the norm in recent years, reflected in the rise of civil law suits, sometimes on outrageous grounds. We have rights and we are not afraid to use them!

In addition to the military use we saw yesterday, the Greek word 'submit' also has a sense of voluntarily giving up our rights for the benefit of others. Although this may not be a popular practice today, it is to just such submission that God calls His people.

Back in Genesis 3, when Adam willingly ate the forbidden fruit, rebellion came into the world. Ultimately all sin is rebellion against God, and in the midst of a rebellious world we who are Christians are called to model true submission. We are to get in line under the worldly authorities that God has put in place whether in the home, the workplace or in society in general, and we are to voluntarily give up our rights, our wants and our desires for the good of others. 'Whoever exalts himself', said Jesus, 'will be humbled, and whoever humbles himself will be exalted' (Matt. 23:12). As we humble ourselves through our voluntary submission, God gives us grace and raises us up.

This may sound all very well in theory, but humbling ourselves is not always that simple and while we may be happy to submit to and give up our rights for those we deem worthy, there will always be others who do not fit that description. This is where our humility is really tested and where we need to remember that all submission is ultimately submission to God.

# > < Reflection

'Whatever' has become the motto of the complacent. 'Do whatever you want.' 'Have whatever you want.' 'Whatever! It's all the same to me.' And the 'whatever' party tend to be of the opinion that by just going with the flow, they are somehow exercising godly submission.

But submission is not the same as complacency – it is not a passive practice undertaken without consideration or contribution. Submission requires our active involvement. How else can it be of value in shaping our lives and our interaction with others?

submission

'Do nothing out of selfish ambition or vain conceit, but in humility consider others better than yourselves.'
**Philippians 2:3**

Some people simply *are* better than us – they have better jobs, wear better clothes, drive better cars, possess better intellect, have better skills. There are always people who seem better than us! But how can we 'consider' people better than us, when we do not believe they are? Is it really possible to submit to people we do not even like or trust?

As with anything, submission takes practice, and in Ephesians 5, Paul lists three specific areas of submission as our training ground:

1. *The submission of a wife to her husband.* Not a licence for husbands to be tyrants, but a request for the voluntary submission of a wife to her husband.

2. *The submission of children to their parents.*

3. *The submission of slaves to their masters.* Though this is no longer a normal practice in modern households, it was a universal part of home life in the Roman empire.

The point Paul is making here is that, as with many areas of Christian life, the practice of submission must begin in the home. If we share our living space with other people, whether family or otherwise, this is our prime training ground for exercising submission.

The home, however, is not the only place we can practise submission. To the church in Rome, Paul declared: 'Everyone must submit himself to the governing authorities, for there is no authority except that which God has established' (Rom. 13:1).

There are ample opportunities for submission to be found in our work places, schools, colleges, universities, clubs, councils and any one of a hundred other organisations or situations in which we might find ourselves. In almost all our interaction with other people we are presented with opportunities to choose to submit.

And then, of course, there is the local church. The Bible not only calls us to submit to church leaders (Heb. 13:17), but also to one another. On the face of it this seems like a ludicrous command – surely if we all submit to each other, we will, in a sense, be stuck forever outside the door waving one another in first. As with Bible study, we find the answer in our relationship with God. If we are to practise submission without causing confusion we need to seek the guidance of the Holy Spirit.

## Application »

Twenty-Four Hour Submission: For one day this week choose, within reason, to submit to everyone. The aim of this is not necessarily to learn submission, but to see how you react and how it makes you feel. Open doors for people. Let other drivers have the right of way, even when officially it is yours. Offer your food to others. If anyone asks something of you that is within your power and not contrary to law or Scripture, do it.

submission

'Slaves, submit yourselves to your masters with all respect, not only to those who are good and considerate, but also to those who are harsh.'

**1 Peter 2:18**

This seems a strange request. In the Roman Empire, slaves had no choice but to submit to their masters, especially since they could have their slaves crucified for disobedience! Peter hardly needed to remind slaves to submit to their masters, but he did need to qualify that submission as being 'with all respect'. What Peter had in view here was the heart of the slaves – their attitude to submission.

While I do not have any slaves at my house, I do have children. I certainly do not equate children with slaves, but I do expect them to submit to my requests. Most have to do with such everyday tasks as keeping their bedrooms tidy or helping out around the house. Hardly excessive and yet so often these requests are met with arguments, sulking or even tears, as though I was some harsh oppressor. They may well do the task asked of them, but it is very rarely with *real* submission. Just because we outwardly submit to others, it does not necessarily mean that we are truly practising submission.

How do we feel when we submit to others? What is our attitude to the thought of submitting to our spouses, our parents, our teachers, our bosses, our church leaders or the government? We may well have no problem with submitting to most of those in positions of authority, or at least the ones who exercise that authority well. The problem comes when we are faced with someone to whom we simply do not want to submit. Maybe we feel they should not have authority. Maybe they do not always agree with us or do things the way we would do them. Maybe we simply do not like them. It is at this point that our willingness to submit is put to the test.

What we are tackling here is our pride – the desire to have our own way, to be important, and not be told what we can or cannot do! At such times we are faced with a choice. Will we voluntarily submit to others or will we resist them? Actually, that is not really the choice, as all submission is ultimately to God. The real choice is: will we rebel against God's rule, or will we submit to Him through this person, and so humble ourselves before Him?

## > < **Reflection**

In Isaac Asimov's three laws of robotics, a robot had to obey orders even if they resulted in its own destruction. The same should *not* be true of us! We need to be wise and get the right balance in submission and avoid it becoming self-destructive. We are called to voluntarily give up our rights and desires for others, ultimately for God's glory, but He is not glorified by us becoming mats for people to walk all over.

## Day 5
## Ultimate Submission

submission

'Pilate said, "Don't you realise I have power either to free you or to crucify you?" Jesus answered, "You would have no power over me if it were not given to you from above."'
**John 19:10–11**

Picture the scene. On the one hand there stands the Roman procurator, the Emperor's representative in Judea. He holds sway over a powerful army and has the authority to sentence his subjects to the most horrific of deaths. On the other hand there stands Jesus, His Father's representative on earth. He holds sway over the armies of God and has authority over the entirety of the physical and spiritual realm. Who should be submitting to whom in this scenario? Which of these men should be lying on his face in the dust at the feet of his superior? It is with true dramatic irony that Pilate faces Jesus and points out that he has power over Him. And yet, rather than call down fire from heaven on this insolent Gentile upstart, Jesus submits to the procurator's authority – even to being scourged, humiliated and nailed on a cross to die!

Throughout His ministry, Jesus modelled submission to the worldly authorities. He paid the required taxes to Rome, giving to Caesar what was Caesar's, even if He did get the money out of a fish! At His trial, He yielded to the interrogation of the high priest, Annas, and even apologised when He inadvertently failed to show Annas the respect due to one in his position. He even submitted as fists punched His face, as thorns dug into His scalp, as whips slashed at His back, and as nails cut through His hands.

Yet it is in His response to Pilate that we see beyond the mere human level of Jesus' submission: 'You would have no power over me if it were not given to you from above.' Though in one sense He submitted Himself to the procurator's authority, in reality He was submitting to the One who *gave* Pilate that authority: God Himself.

Paul makes this point clear in his letter to the Philippians, saying that, in submission to the Father, Jesus 'made himself nothing, taking the very nature of a servant, being made in human likeness. And being found in appearance as a man, he humbled himself and became obedient to death – even death on a cross!' (Phil. 2:7–8).

As a carpenter, Jesus knew all about wood and nails, and in the end He used them to demonstrate ultimate submission to God!

## > < Reflection

We have considered our submission to others, whether in the home, in society or in the Church. We have looked at our ultimate submission to God as the One who has supreme authority. In addition we are called to submit to the Word of God.

Last week we saw that the Bible is our ultimate authority, and as we study our Bibles in submission so we learn to live more for God's glory.

**1.** What response does the word 'submission' produce in you?

**2.** All submission is ultimately to God. Why do you think God demands and deserves our submission?

**3.** Read James 4:6–8. How does submitting to others (whether worldly authorities or others in the Church) fulfil this call to submit to God?

**4.** If you tried the Twenty-Four Hour Submission (see page 25), how did it make you feel? What aspect did you find hardest?

**5.** If you did not try it, what made you make that decision?

**6.** How would you describe the relationship between fellowship and submission?

**7.** If a non-Christian asked why you believe biblical submission is a good thing, what would you say?

submission

# WEEK 3: FOCUS ON OURSELVES
# giving

GIVING

www.cwr.org.uk/vital

## Introduction

'Will a man rob God? Yet you rob me. But you ask, "How do we rob you?" In tithes and offerings.' **Malachi 3:8**

There tends to be an air of suspicion around the topic of Christian giving. Those outside the Church seem to assume we are obligated to support the Church financially, like some kind of pyramid scheme or co-operative. Even Christians can be somewhat wary when faced with sermons on this topic. 'Why are we hearing about giving again?' we may ask ourselves. 'What do they need money for this time? And more importantly, how much is it going to cost me?'

Sometimes such questions are fully justified, especially when verses like the one from Malachi above and terms like 'sacrificial giving' and 'double-tithing' start getting thrown around. This can lead not only to a degree of uneasiness, but also confusion and misunderstanding about true Christian giving.

As we turn our focus on ourselves in this third week of studies, we are looking at the area of discipline called 'giving' or 'stewardship'. It is probably one of the most common or at least regular practices that Christians engage in, but is it really fulfilling its purpose in growing our love for God?

We will be looking not only at how giving shapes us, but also what it involves, why it is important and how to practically engage in this vital area of spiritual discipline.

'But now, by dying to what once bound us, we have been released from the law so that we serve in the new way of the Spirit, and not in the old way of the written code.'
**Romans 7:6**

This may seem an odd place to start when tackling the subject of giving. But since so much teaching on giving is built on the old covenant, we need to address this before we look at true Christian giving.

Since the King James version of the Bible rose to popularity, 'tithing' has become almost synonymous with 'giving' in the Church. It is an Old English word that simply means 'tenth', and the annual giving of a tenth was related to the promised land: 'A tithe of everything from the land, whether grain from the soil or fruit from the trees, belongs to the LORD; it is holy to the LORD' (Lev. 27:30).

The tithing law is defined more clearly in Deuteronomy 14, but we could sum up its main points as follows:

+ The people were to give a tenth of everything produced from or raised on the land (crops and livestock).

+ It did not include money, time, services or manufactured goods.

+ Two out of three years the tithe was taken to Jerusalem for a national feast.

giving

+ In the third year it was stored up in towns and cities to provide for those with no land of their own.

Based on this, it is fairly clear that the tithing law could hardly be considered a model for Christian giving!

The writer to the Hebrews describes the whole of the Jewish law as 'obsolete' (Heb. 8:13), and as Paul stresses in Romans, Christians are not under the law – no part of it binds us today. Christian living only *looks* like we obey some of the law. In England we obey laws that are similar to those in France, but no one takes this to mean we are subject to French law! As far as the ten per cent is concerned, we are one hundred per cent free from it. Instead of following a list of rules, Paul points out that Christians are to be led by the Holy Spirit in all they do, including giving. Christian giving is about seeking God's guidance and obeying Him.

# > < Reflection

Sermons on Christian giving almost always focus on money and the Bible certainly has plenty to say about it. But we are stewards of so much more than this.

In his first letter to Timothy, Paul wrote, 'we brought nothing into the world, and we can take nothing out of it' (1 Tim. 6:7). We were born with nothing – no clothes or possessions, no skills or knowledge, only our bodies and time, and even these we did not work for or earn.

Take a moment to consider the things you have at your disposal. You are the steward of everything you have and all these things can be used in the practice of giving.

# You Can't Out-Give God!

> 'Heal the sick, raise the dead, cleanse those who have leprosy, drive out demons. Freely you have received, freely give.'
> **Matthew 10:8**

giving

'Simony' is the practice of buying or selling spiritual benefits such as positions in the Church or pardon for sin. It is named after Simon the sorcerer who appears in Acts 8 offering money to Peter and John in return for the ability to zap people with the Holy Spirit! Unsurprisingly Peter and John turned him down: 'May your money perish with you, because you thought you could buy the gift of God with money!' (Acts 8:20). And while this may seem a bit harsh, they had been among the twelve disciples that Jesus had sent out with the command to 'freely give'.

Matthew tells us that Jesus 'gave them authority to drive out evil spirits and to heal every disease and sickness' (Matt. 10:1). The disciples had not asked for the ability to perform such miracles, though undoubtedly they would have relished it! Jesus just *gave* them the authority and that was that – it was a free gift to them and He told them not to charge others for its use.

In a sense our possessions *do* belong to us. Earlier in Acts, when rebuking Ananias for lying about how much money he got for his land, Peter said, 'Didn't it belong to you before it was sold? And after it was sold, wasn't the money at your disposal?' (Acts 5:4). His land. His money. But yesterday we read that 'we brought nothing into the world, and we can take nothing out of it' (1 Tim. 6:7).

If God had not given them to us we would have no skills or abilities, no money or possessions, no food, no water, no time, no life. We may have worked hard for the things we have, but ultimately we received them *freely*. Our aim in giving is not to try to repay God – as the saying goes, 'you cannot out-give God'! But we can use our resources to invest in His kingdom. And as we seek first His kingdom (Matt. 6:33), God has promised to keep providing for us, not only with the material things we need for life, but with treasure stored up for us in heaven! How much better to contribute to God's work in the world through giving, than to squander what we have on ourselves.

# > < Reflection

In the Sermon on the Mount, Jesus taught on giving, or rather on how *not* to give:

'... when you give to the needy, do not announce it with trumpets ... to be honoured by men' (Matt. 6:2).

When we give, we are merely using the things we have been given ourselves. God does not *only* own the cattle on a thousand hills, but declares, 'The world is mine, and all that is in it' (Psa. 50:12).

Can we really be proud or boastful about giving something that isn't really ours?

'On the first day of every week, each one of you should set aside a sum of money in keeping with his income, saving it up, so that when I come no collections will have to be made.'
**1 Corinthians 16:2**

When advising the Corinthian church, Paul recommended they take the time to plan their giving carefully. As we have already seen, it is not about following a set of rules, but working together with the Holy Spirit. We need to seek His guidance in a practical way, asking Him:

+ *When to give:* Paul suggests the Corinthians set aside money on the first day of every week, not because that was payday (workers in the Roman Empire were usually paid daily), but because that was when they came together to worship God – an ideal time to seek Him and take a collection. While we should be ready to give at all times, it is worth including this question in your daily prayers.

+ *What to give:* when it comes to money, the question may simply be how much to give, but we have seen that giving is about more than just money. You may be financially poor, but rich in time or skills etc. Asking *what* to give is an important question, as God may want you to provide for someone in a way you had not previously considered.

+ *To whom to give:* another important point that is often overlooked is the recipient of our giving. The usual practice is simply to give to the local church and allow the leaders to sort out what to do with it.

giving

But if we are to be good stewards of all we have, we need to ask God to show us to whom He wants us to give, being open to follow His leading.

In his first letter, John wrote, 'If anyone has material possessions and sees his brother in need but has no pity on him, how can the love of God be in him?' (1 John 3:17). In addition to the questions above, we need to be constantly on the look out for opportunities to give to those in need.

Not only that, but remember others may be looking to give as well. While we might be inclined to conceal *our* needs, this is really a reflection of our pride and independence. But if we let people know when we are struggling and in need, it gives others an opportunity to use their God-given gifts as well.

## Application »

This week, take time each day to ask the Holy Spirit to help you practise giving. If you have a spouse or prayer partner, it may be worth doing this together with them to check you have heard correctly. Then act on what He says, bearing in mind: 'Each man should give what he has decided in his heart to give, not reluctantly or under compulsion, for God loves a cheerful giver' (2 Cor. 9:7).

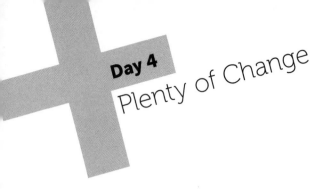

'Give, and it will be given to you. A good measure, pressed down, shaken together and running over, will be poured into your lap. For with the measure you use, it will be measured to you.'
**Luke 6:38**

giving

Like many people, I love testimonies that remind me God is at work in people's lives. Even the 'I prayed and God gave me a parking space' ones work for me! I do however become a little wary at testimonies where someone has given money to some cause or other and has immediately received some kind of financial return, such as a tax rebate or an inheritance. My concern is not whether God does such things, but rather what message is being communicated.

The preaching of the 'prosperity gospel' is still very popular, with its promise that when we give financially to a specific church or ministry, God will increase our material wealth. True Christian giving, whether it is financial or otherwise, should not be about seeking a greater return in kind. God may reward us in such a way, but it cannot be our motivation. Our incentive should be based on our desire to grow in our love for God, and the practice of giving assists in a number of ways:

+ *Giving helps us guard our hearts.* The Bible has much to say about the danger of being enslaved by money, as 'You cannot serve both God and Money' (Matt. 6:24). We cannot serve God and *any* possession, and giving helps us not to get caught in idolatry.

+ *Giving helps us recognise the Holy Spirit's voice.* Giving, like Bible study and submission, requires the guidance of the Holy Spirit, and as we seek and follow His leading so we learn to discern when He is speaking.

+ *Giving helps us get involved in God's work.* While we may feel like we are not as useful to God as we might be, giving is one way we can all get involved in the work of serving Him and furthering His kingdom.

As with all spiritual discipline, we give because of our relationship with God; as Paul told the Corinthians, giving is 'the proof of your love' (2 Cor. 8:24).

# Application »

A few weeks ago, I came home to find that my garden had been transformed. The toys that are usually strewn about the place had been gathered together neatly. The lawn was no longer a swaying jungle, but was neatly cropped. Even my hedge, which was in danger of becoming a row of trees, had been tamed. I found out later than someone from my church had given his time to come and sort out my garden, and while you might consider this an invasion of privacy, I have never made any secret about my distaste for gardening. I was really blessed!

Have a look at your schedule for the next week and set aside as much time as possible to bless someone in your church or neighbourhood. Ask God to inspire you and show you the who, how and when.

# The Lord, The Giver of Life

giving

'For you know the grace of our Lord Jesus Christ, that though he was rich, yet for your sakes he became poor, so that you through his poverty might become rich.'
**2 Corinthians 8:9**

Jesus not only taught about giving, He also exemplified it in His life, constantly giving what He had to bless and provide for others. The Gospel writers regularly zoom in on Jesus' interaction with individuals, detailing the time and attention He gave them despite being constantly busy and in demand. He gave time to speak with the Samaritan woman at the well (John 4:1–26). He was willing to touch the leper who had been rejected by everyone else (Matt. 8:1–4). He stopped to identify the bleeding woman who had touched Him (Matt. 9:20–22), and took a huge detour, even leaving Palestine, to visit the Syrophoenician Woman (Matt. 15:21–28). In addition to His time, Jesus gave the other things He had. He shared His knowledge and wisdom, and His message of the coming kingdom of God; He used His gift of healing, and He even raised the dead to serve those with whom He came into contact.

But as we zoom out to consider the bigger picture, we see Jesus' supreme example of giving! Next week I will tell you my favourite verse in the Bible, but most people's is probably John 3:16: 'For God so loved the world that he gave his one and only Son, that whoever believes in him shall not perish but have eternal life.' Note the word 'gave' in there, and Paul called Jesus, 'the Son of God, who loved me and *gave* himself for me' (Gal. 2:20, my empahasis). Jesus gave us Himself.

Though He is God, He became human, living in mediocrity for thirty years before embarking on a three-year mission that led to Him being executed in the most brutal method imaginable. He did not give only ten per cent of Himself, but one hundred per cent – everything He had, He gave up for us. And He did this not out of compulsion but out of choice, because of His great love for us and submission to the Father.

It is true – we really cannot out-give God! But in love we *can* give what we have for His glory and His kingdom.

# Application ››

While writing this book, I gave away my rather eclectic collection of vinyl records to a friend. Although they had spent the last ten years stored away in my loft, doing nothing but gather dust and spiders, I could not bring myself to part with them. It was ludicrous really as I have not owned a record player for years! Giving them away, though, was good for me – the hold they had on me, although relatively light, was broken, and my friend seemed to appreciate them. Well, some of them!

What treasures have you got stashed away that do not get as much use as they could? If you have such things, ask God if these might bless others and enjoy the thrill of giving them away!

**1.** Consider times in your life when you have benefited from Christians giving you their time, money or other resources.

**2.** Read Romans 13:7 and 1 Timothy 5:8. What do these two verses have to say about how we prioritise what we do with our money?

**3.** When asked for money by a beggar, Peter told him, 'Silver or gold I do not have, but what I have I give you' (Acts 3:6). Apart from money, what other things might you be able to give to provide for and bless others?

**4.** Read Romans 7:6. Taking the time to enquire of and listen to the Holy Spirit is an essential part of knowing what, when and to whom we should give. How does this work in practice? And how can you be sure you have heard correctly?

**5.** Jesus said, 'It is more blessed to give than to receive' (Acts 20:35). In what way do you think there might be greater blessing in giving than in receiving?

**6.** While we may bless others by giving, we can also bless them by receiving. How might you go about letting others in your church know that you are struggling or in need?

**7.** The subject of 'giving' is one that non-Christians tend to be suspicious about. How would you explain to such a person why giving is important and what it involves?

giving

# WEEK 4: FOCUS ON DAILY LIFE
# giving thanks

## Introduction

'Give thanks to the LORD, for he is good. *His love endures for ever.* Give thanks to the God of gods. *His love endures for ever.* Give thanks to the Lord of lords: *His love endures for ever.'*
**Psalm 136:1–3**

Gratitude is one of the most basic ingredients of human interaction. It is so basic, in fact, that often we do not even need to think about saying 'thank you' – it is almost instinctive. And when it is lacking its absence is glaringly obvious in its rudeness!

Because it is so basic, though, giving thanks may seem oddly out of place among the other areas of spiritual discipline covered in this series.

How can we compare showing God a bit of appreciation with the great labours of Bible study, submission and giving?

Is thanksgiving really of any genuine value in our walk with God, beyond preventing us from being inadvertently impolite to the Lord of the universe?

Having looked last week at giving our time and other resources in service to God, now we turn our attention to giving Him our thanks. We will consider the purpose of thanksgiving and the reasons for thanking God, how to engage in this practically and why its regular practice is important – so important, in fact, that thanksgiving is part of our focus on daily life.

giving thanks

'Always giving thanks
to God the Father
for everything, in the
name of our Lord
Jesus Christ.'
**Ephesians 5:20**

While I cannot immediately recall the first words of
my four children, I can guarantee none of them was
'thank you'. Even now, though they all speak English
fairly fluently, expressions of gratitude rarely make an
appearance without a degree of prompting.

Contrary to what they may think, it is not because
my children do not have anything to be thankful for.
They just seem not to realise it, either because they
are too absorbed in what they are doing or because
they simply expect to be provided for and treated in a
certain way.

Saying 'thank you' is not as natural a reaction for
most people as we might think – it takes thought
and effort. This is no less true when it comes to our
relationship with God. So while it is fairly easy to work
out what 'giving thanks' is, actually *doing* it is not
quite so simple. It is something we have to work at and
exercise in order for it to become more instinctive. Not
only that, but when we come across verses like the
one above from Ephesians and read Paul using words
like 'always' and 'for everything' when talking about
giving thanks to God, it may seem on the face of it to
be somewhat extreme. Surely if we actually did this,
we would be too busy saying 'thank you' to have time
to experience anything to be grateful for!

This word 'always', however, does not necessarily have a sense of constant, unending action. If I say, 'I always put milk in my coffee', this does not mean I spend my every waking moment pouring milk. It might be better translated 'on every occasion', or as Paul puts it in his first letter to the Thessalonians, 'give thanks *in all circumstances*' (1 Thess. 5:18, my emphasis).

When it comes to spiritual discipline, then, real thanksgiving is not reflected in occasional expressions of gratitude to God nor in the emission of a constant stream of 'thank you's. Rather it has to do with developing a mindset of giving thanks to God in all circumstances so that, in whatever situation we find ourselves, whether good, bad or indifferent, our automatic reaction is to see His hand of love at work and respond in gratitude.

# Application »

While looking at giving last week, we saw that though we may have worked hard for the things we have, ultimately we received them freely as gifts from God. The food we eat, the clothes we wear, the people we meet, the skills we acquire, our possessions, our knowledge, our abilities and even the air we breathe all come from God.

Write out a list of those things you have for which you are most grateful, and as you do so take a few moments to say 'thank you' to God for each one, acknowledging that they are all gifts He has given you.

# Grateful For Everything

'And we know that in all things God works for the good of those who love him, who have been called according to his purpose.'
**Romans 8:28**

## giving thanks

I promised to let you know what my favourite Bible verse is. Well, this is it – one of the most amazing promises in Scripture. Again and again I come back to this statement, especially when life is not going quite the way I had hoped it would, which is fairly often. What encouragement there is in these few words; what consolation!

Take a moment to consider what this verse promises. The Creator of the universe, the One who knows the beginning from the end, who has supreme power and authority, is working all things for good. Not just the good things or even the moderately okay things, but *all* things – even the most horrific of events and distressing of experiences. And since this promise comes from God, I have to believe that when all is said and done and everything that has ever happened is placed on the scales, they will not tip only slightly in favour of 'good'. Surely the good that God is working out will be so overwhelmingly greater, it will utterly eclipse all that is bad or negative! For this reason, then, we really can give thanks in all circumstances.

Sometimes thanksgiving is hard for the simple fact that life may seem to lack anything to be thankful for. For much of this year I have suffered with depression, which on some days has left me staring for hours at the wall, unable to do, say or even think about anything in particular. At such times thanksgiving seemed completely alien to me. Why give thanks when life is so grey and empty? Even if I wanted to, what on earth was there to thank God for? Yet even times of misery, adversity and desolation are included in this sweeping promise that God works 'all things' for the good of those who love Him. And let's not forget that our prime goal in spiritual discipline is to do just that.

## Application »

While the things you struggle with may be completely different from mine, we all experience hardship of one kind or another. Jesus made this clear to His followers saying, 'In this world you will have trouble'. It is inescapable – part and parcel of life in this fallen world. Yet He continued with the declaration, 'But take heart! I have overcome the world' (John 16:33).

Take a moment to think about one of the struggles in your life at the moment. It does not matter if it is something big or small, something that comes immediately to mind or takes a while to identify, but when you have thought of it consider God's promise to use even this struggle for your good and the good of others. Even if you cannot imagine how this is possible, accept His promise in faith and give Him thanks!

giving thanks

'The one who offers thanksgiving as his sacrifice glorifies me.'
**Psalm 50:23 ESV**

'Sacrifice' is an emotive word. For me it conjures up images of WWI soldiers fighting in the trenches or parents in war torn countries shielding their children with their bodies, of Aztec priests hurling people into flames or streams of blood running down altar stones. It suggests pain and death, fear and loss. In what way, then, is thanksgiving a sacrifice?

Consider some of the things we have seen in the last two days – the call to give thanks in all circumstances, to develop a mindset of thanksgiving, even to respond to difficult and painful situations with gratitude to God. Such things are not easy and do not come naturally to us, and so engaging in thanksgiving requires a certain amount of self-sacrifice and diligent practice.

As with all areas of spiritual discipline, it is best to start out simple, and where better to begin than at the dinner table? If you are asked to 'give thanks' here it does not need any qualification or explanation – we know it is a request to thank God for the food, to say 'grace'. This is one of the most common times to give thanks, and as we all need to eat regularly, this potentially provides us with many opportunities to exercise thanksgiving every day!

Another great time to practise giving thanks is at the end of each day, which is why I have included this in the focus on daily life. It does not need to be a lengthy activity, saying 'thank you' for every little thing that has happened, but simply taking a few minutes before you settle down to sleep to look back over your day and take the opportunity to thank God for the things you remember. What good things come to mind? What difficult things? Even if you cannot see how God might use them for good, receive in faith God's promise to do so. Giving thanks not only for the big incidents but also the little things is important, as the aim is to develop a tendency and habit to look out for opportunities to thank God continually throughout the day.

At first, it will seem like a sacrifice, but as we pursue this area of spiritual discipline, our growing predisposition to offer thanksgiving no matter what the circumstance really will glorify God.

## Application >>

'Practice makes perfect'. At least that is what we are told, though I cannot recall it ever really being proven. That said, I can certainly testify that, whether it is applied to learning a musical instrument, taking up a new hobby or developing a particular skill, practice does at least make *better*!

The same is true of thanksgiving. At the end of each day for the next week, spend a few minutes going over the events of the day in your mind and try to come up with at least five things for which you can thank God.

## Day 4
## Living by Faith

'They ... order them to abstain from certain foods, which God created to be received with thanksgiving by those who believe and who know the truth. For everything God created is good, and nothing is to be rejected if it is received with thanksgiving.'
**1 Timothy 4:3–4**

Was it okay to eat the meat of animals that had been sacrificed to idols? This was one of the burning issues in the Early Church which Paul had to address on a number of occasions. Although not that relevant to us today, we can easily imagine the dilemma. Here were people who had grown up worshipping idols and watching priests offer them sacrifices, but now their lives had been transformed – they had found the one true God and rejected their old false gods. Then they saw other Christians eating the meat of those sacrificed animals. What were they to think about this? We might compare the situation to a reformed alcoholic struggling with the idea of taking real wine at communion, or a convert from Islam wrestling with whether or not to accept an invitation to an event held in a mosque.

Paul's response to this challenge was to explain to the churches in his care that all things ultimately come from God, even meat offered to idols, and so everything may be accepted. Our task then, rather than to reject such questionable items, is to receive them in faith as gifts from God, and our faith in this is demonstrated by our grateful response to Him.

Thanksgiving, then, helps us to exercise and build up our faith in God's provision – not just of meat offered to idols or those things we judge to be good, but of *all* things. Even if we are not feeling especially grateful, giving thanks to God for what He has given us and all He has done helps us to realise that God is at work at all times in our lives.

As you can see, this a great exercise in faith – particularly when giving thanks for difficult or unpleasant situations and events – and the more we make this sacrifice of thanksgiving, the more our eyes will be opened to the reality of God's work, and so we will increasingly trust Him.

# > < Reflection

Today was a fairly typical mix of events. I spent some time tidying the house with my family, helped my oldest son with a school project, discovered an expensive-looking leak in my roof, watched a film while eating dinner and spent the evening out with a couple of friends. There were no major decisions made, no great catastrophes, no unexpected revelations – nothing especially noteworthy. And yet who knows how significant any of these events might be?

So whether they seem good, bad or somewhere in between, I am going to end today in thanksgiving, in faith that through it all God has been working out His plan both in my life and the lives of those around me.

# When He Gave Thanks ...

## giving thanks

'And [Jesus] took bread, gave thanks and broke it, and gave it to them, saying, "This is my body given for you; do this in remembrance of me."'
**Luke 22:19**

At first it is something of a surprise to discover that the Gospels rarely record Jesus giving thanks. In fact they mention only four specific occasions. Though we assume Jesus gave thanks frequently, the Gospel writers seem more interested in the 'how' of His thanksgiving than the 'how often'.

Consider then those four occasions of thanksgiving:

+ Jesus spoke to a crowd of 5,000 people and called on His disciples to feed them (Matt. 14:13–21). After complaining a bit, they managed to come up with a handful of bread and a few fishes – a meal for a child. On receiving this food, however, Jesus gave thanks for it, and suddenly it multiplied so that everyone was fed, with plenty left over. A similar incident is recorded later with a crowd of four thousand people (Mark 8:1–13).

+ Jesus' friend, Lazarus, had died suddenly and been laid to rest in his tomb. Standing in front of it, Jesus said aloud, 'Father, I thank you that you have heard me' (John 11:41). No sooner had He uttered this prayer of thanksgiving than He called for Lazarus to 'come forth' and the once dead man did just that!

+ On the night He was betrayed, Jesus gathered His disciples to share in the Passover meal together. We are told He gave thanks to God for both the bread and the wine before passing them to the others, and in this way He instituted the great memorial of the new covenant – Communion – that Christians around the world have given thanks for and eaten together ever since.

+ Finally, after the resurrection, some of His followers invited Jesus into their house in Emmaus, although they had not yet recognised that it was Him (Luke 24:28–35). At the table, He gave thanks for the bread and began to dish it out to them, when suddenly their eyes were opened and they realised that He was Jesus, risen from the dead!

Jesus gave thanks for food, drink and for being heard by God – all normal, everyday phenomena. And yet despite this He clearly understood that even these most simple of things can have great significance. His example to us is straightforward: give thanks for all things!

# > < Reflection

Whether, like my children, we expect to be provided for or treated in a certain way, we can still choose to give thanks to God for everything we have and everything we go through. Thanksgiving has not so much to do with us as it has to do with God. It is a choice, an act of our will to put our faith in Him.

As the author, G. K. Chesterton, wrote, 'When it comes to life the critical thing is whether you take things for granted or take them with gratitude.'* Which will you choose?

• Chesterton, G. K. *Irish Impressions*, (London: Collins & Sons, 1919) p.24

**1.** If a Sunday school class asked you to explain how to give thanks, what would you say?

**2.** In what way might thanksgiving be thought of as a 'sacrifice'?

**3.** Read Romans 8:28. Consider some of the struggles that you or those you know have gone through, which maybe seemed bad at the time, but in hindsight prove this promise from God.

**4.** What is the difference between being fatalistic, and believing that God uses everything, whether seemingly good or bad, for ultimate good?

**5.** There are a number of hymns and Christian songs that prompt us with reasons to be thankful to God. Consider whether you have found any of these helpful, and how they have encouraged you to give thanks.

**6.** Read Romans 5:10. Why do you think Christians often find it hard to give thanks despite the fact that Jesus died for us and so our lives should be overflowing with gratitude and love for God?

**7.** While the concept of thanksgiving is simple, how would you explain to another Christian why it is important, and what advice would you give to help them give thanks to the Lord?

make it a habit

giving thanks

# Leader's notes:

These notes are designed to help with the 'Questions for Consideration or Discussion' and may be used for individual study or for leading these sessions in a group.

## Introductory Questions - page 6

1. This is a very important point that is fundamental to the Christian life. It may help to look at the verses that talk about us loving Him (eg Exod. 20:6; Rom. 8:28; 1 Cor. 2:9; James 1:12) as well as the many verses that talk about His love for us.

2. to 5. It may be worth writing down what you understand to be the purpose and practice of these four areas of discipline. It does not need to be an exhaustive description, perhaps just a list of bullet points or a couple of sentences. You can then refer back to these in the next few weeks to see if your understanding of them has changed.

6. The focus here is specifically on your experience of these four areas of spiritual discipline. If you are leading a small group, sharing personal examples may encourage others as well.

7. Note that in these verses the transformation happens *to* us rather than being something done *by* us. It may help to look for other verses that speak about God's role and our role.

To help you identify times when you have worked in partnership with God, consider times in your life when you have experienced real inner transformation.

Again, if you are leading a small group preparing some personal examples in advance may help.

1. Consider first whether you engage in frequent Bible study. If not, there must be a reason behind this, whether it has to do with time, inclination, capacity or capability.

If you are leading a small group, it is worth sharing your own struggles (if any) to encourage others to contribute.

2. This is not a simple question, but it does deserve consideration. If you are struggling, try to think about the big picture – the overview of Scripture. Whether you see the Bible as a message of God's love and forgiveness, His salvation plan, His desire to make a people for Himself, or something else, this is about how *you* see it, so there is no specific, correct answer.

3. Note the verbs in this verse used to describe the Holy Spirit's work. The issue is not 'Does He guide and speak to us?' It is 'Can we identify when He does so?'

Again, if you are leading a small group, be prepared to share your own experiences to get the ball rolling.

4. Bible study aids can take many forms – commentaries, study Bibles, Bible guides, study guides, lecture and sermon recordings, concordances, Hebrew and Greek Bibles, devotional material and so on. If you have not used anything like these, it is worth asking other Christians, whose insight into Scripture you respect, what study aids they use. It would be a shame to miss out on the wealth of study material that has been handed down through the centuries!

Bible study

5. As I mentioned, I am an auditory learner so I take information in best through hearing. For this reason, I tend to read Scripture aloud or listen to audio recordings of the Bible, of which there are many.

If you are not sure which way of studying is most effective for you, there are tests available on the internet.

6. This is considered further in the study 'Meditation: focus on God'.

7. There is a saying, 'you don't really know something unless you can explain it', and the aim of this question is to ensure you have a proper knowledge and understanding of Bible study.

If you are part of a small group, it may be worth turning this into a role-playing exercise so each person gets to explain the purpose of Bible study to another.

1. Consider both your general reaction to the thought of submission, and how you feel about the specific idea of submitting to the people in authority over you and others in your local church.

This is not meant to give you a sense of failure or condemnation – it is natural to feel a certain amount of aversion to this, especially when thinking about submission to people we do not like or respect.

2. A fairly straightforward question since He is God, but it is worth spending some time looking at what the Bible says about His desire for submission. It may help to start with the following verses: Exodus 20:1–6, Psalm 8:3–4 and Isaiah 55:8–11.

3. This is an important concept to work through, as the call to submit to worldly authorities and others in the Church is not easy, and there will be times when we need to be really certain that it *is* important and that we are ultimately submitting to God.

4. and 5. These questions relate to the application section on Day 3 (page 25).

If you are leading a small group it is worth trying the Twenty-Four Hour Submission yourself and sharing your experiences and how it made you feel.

6. The study 'Fellowship: focus on God' looks at the fact that true fellowship is more than just spending social time with other believers – it is about sharing our lives with one another, supporting, caring for, providing for and generally loving others in our Christian community. Bearing this in mind, it may help

submission

to consider how submission might help promote such fellowship.

7. As submission is often considered a weakness or at least distasteful to most people, it is worth considering how you would defend this area of spiritual discipline to a non-Christian. Assume a general lack of biblical knowledge and understanding of Christian jargon as you seek to explain the purpose of biblical submission.

Another read through of Day 2 and Day 4 may also help.

# Week 3: Giving – page 42

1. If you are leading a small group, it may be worth sharing some examples from your own life to encourage others to share.

2. These verses talk about the need to pay our debts and to provide for our families. These are an important part of godly stewardship and need to be taken into account as part of this area of spiritual discipline. If, as a result of our giving, we fail to pay our debts as agreed or to provide for those in our families, how is that in any way honouring to God?

3. Do not get too specific when listing the various things you might be able to give – the aim here is to take the time to look at the things you have that are not merely financial.

Note that Peter did not give the beggar any specific possession, but instead used his gift of healing. When considering the things you have, include non-material things such as skills and knowledge.

4. This is not only vital for giving, but for *all* areas of spiritual discipline, including Bible study and submission, where our ability to hear and discern the Holy Spirit is fundamental. While God can speak to us in many different ways, the most common way is directly into our thoughts, and being able to work out what *is* His voice and what is *not* is crucial for us if we are going to grow in our relationship with God.

giving

5. Think about your own experiences of giving and receiving, and consider ways in which each has been a blessing. It may be worth looking at giving first and then comparing this with receiving, as this is supposed to produce the greater blessing.

6. There is a tendency, especially in Western society, to keep quiet about our needs and to shun charity. However, since it is important to provide others with the opportunity to give, the aim here is not merely theoretical, but practical – these are things to be put into practice. For example, local church 'Freecycle' groups can be a helpful tool.

If the idea of asking people for things is distasteful to you, think of it as opening yourself up to be a channel of greater blessing for others – it is almost a sacrifice!

7. Again, by considering how you would explain the importance and practice of giving to a non-believer, this will force you to avoid Christian jargon and the assumption of any level of prior knowledge of spiritual discipline.

If you are in a small group, try role-playing this conversation, taking turns at being the non-Christian.

1. By 'Sunday school class' I mean a group of children, say between 5 and 8. At this age children can grasp fairly complex concepts as long as they are expressed in a clear, simple fashion. As such you need to really get to the heart of how to give thanks and what its purpose is.

2. Take into consideration the fact that we are called to give thanks in all circumstances, regardless of whether they appear to be beneficial and whether we feel thankful at the time.

3. This is not always an easy or painless task, but as we look at what God has done in our lives and the lives of others, it really builds our faith to see how He has been at work even through the hardest of times.

If you are leading a small group it may be worth preparing some examples from your own life to encourage others to share.

4. Many Christians adopt a fatalistic, 'que sera sera' (whatever will be will be) attitude to life, believing this is equivalent to trusting in or surrendering to God. But choosing to believe God's promise of Romans 8:28 is much more than this. The aim of this question is to work out what the difference really is.

5. If you are leading a small group, it may be worth thinking of examples to share with the group. It may also be a good opportunity to sing some hymns of thanksgiving together.

giving thanks

5. There may be many reasons we might struggle to give thanks to God, so try to approach this from your own experience: what might prevent you from engaging in thanksgiving?

The aim of this question is to bring us back to the wonderful truth that, no matter how bad life gets, we have the greatest of all reasons to be thankful!

7. Imagine the Christian in question does not think thanksgiving is particularly important and your task is to try to convince them that it is.

If there is more than one of you tackling this question it may be worth role-playing this situation so that you can consider the topic from both sides and hopefully come to a deeper and clearer understanding of the importance of thanksgiving.

Courses and seminars

Publishing and new media

Conference facilities

# Transforming lives

CWR's vision is to enable people to experience personal transformation through applying God's Word to their lives and relationships.

Our Bible-based training and resources help people around the world to:
• Grow in their walk with God
• Understand and apply Scripture to their lives
• Resource themselves and their church
• Develop pastoral care and counselling skills
• Train for leadership
• Strengthen relationships, marriage and family life and much more.

Our insightful writers provide daily Bible-reading notes and other resources for all ages, and our experienced course designers and presenters have gained an international reputation for excellence and effectiveness.

CWR's Training and Conference Centres in Surrey and East Sussex, England, provide excellent facilities in idyllic settings – ideal for both learning and spiritual refreshment.

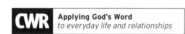

**CWR** Applying God's Word
*to everyday life and relationships*

CWR, Waverley Abbey House,
Waverley Lane, Farnham,
Surrey GU9 8EP, UK

Telephone: **+44 (0)1252 784700**
Email: info@cwr.org.uk
Website: www.cwr.org.uk

Registered Charity No 294387
Company Registration No 1990308